THE BIGGEST EVER BOOK OF PAPER PLANES

With 12 giant
templates for the
biggest paper
air force ever made

NICK ROBINSON

THE BIGGEST
EVER BOOK OF
PAPER PLANES

Ivy Press

First published in the UK in 2009 by
Ivy Press
210 High Street, Lewes
East Sussex BN7 2NS
United Kingdom
www.ivy-group.co.uk

British Library Cataloguing-in-Publication Data
A catalogue record for this book is available from the British Library

ISBN: 978-1-905695-84-3

Ivy Press
This book was conceived, designed and produced by Ivy Press
Creative Director Peter Bridgewater
Publisher Jason Hook
Editorial Director Tom Kitch
Art Director Wayne Blades
Designers Kate Haynes and Andrew Milne
Illustrators Adam Elliott and Michael Howells at Inhouse Design

All designs by Nick Robinson except for the Temko which
is designed by Florence Temko, and the Swallow and Laser
which are adapted from traditional designs by the author.

The author would like to thank his wife Alison, Florence for sharing
her design, David Petty for proofing the diagrams, the British
Origami Society for encouragement and all at Ivy Press for making
this book happen. The author's website is www.origami.me.uk and
he welcomes original designs.

Picture Acknowledgements
Sambrogio, page 9; Dan Barnes, page 13; and Jupiter Images,
page 17.

Printed and bound in China

10 9 8 7 6 5 4 3 2 1

CONTENTS

INTRODUCTION

Using the latest in origami technology and design, each of these 12 planes has specific features that will help you make the most of your paper air force, from vertical fins and dive-bombing capabilities to specialist wingtips and streamlined nose cones, giving you the ultimate performance needed for take-off, attack or simply length of flight. Each plane also has its own weapon and attack capabilities, allowing you to tailor your missions accordingly.

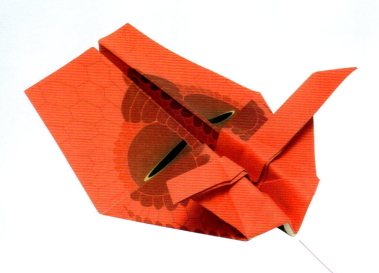

HOW TO USE THIS BOOK

First try to learn the basic designs using plain photocopier paper. Once you can fold these well, move on to the exciting templates at the back of the book. Like any paper, these templates will last longer if kept dry, so be careful of puddles and lakes if launching outdoors. You could even hang the larger planes from your bedroom ceiling for an eye-catching display.

The designs are in order of folding complexity, so if you are new to paper folding, start at the beginning and work your way through in order. Always fold slowly and don't flatten until the paper is perfectly in position. Fold on a large, clear table, with plenty of light to see what you are doing. Please read the section on folding symbols before you start – it will help. Don't forget to read both the diagrams and the words for each project.

FOLDING SYMBOLS

You will find it easy to follow each plane's folding instructions if you learn the simple folding symbols illustrated below. They will also allow you to understand 'normal' origami diagrams.

Valley fold
Fold the paper in the direction of the arrow. Take your time to line the edges up neatly. Hold the paper in place with one hand and put in the crease with the other.

Mountain fold
The paper is folding underneath. It's easiest to turn the paper over and make a valley fold, but remember to turn it back over so the diagrams match the paper.

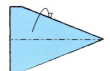 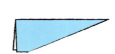

Rotate
Turn the paper 90 degrees in the direction of the arrows.

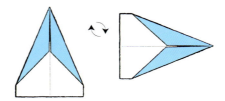

Turn over
Turn the paper upside down, as if you were flipping a pancake.

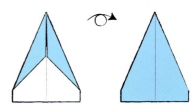

Inside reverse (push in)
A folded corner is pressed inside the paper. Make the initial crease as a valley, then change the creases as shown. Open the body slightly and gently push the corner inside.

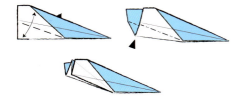

Repeat indicated steps on the other side
Follow the same sequence as before on the opposite side.

Fold to the dotted line
Use the dotted line as a guide to where to fold.

Fold between circled points
The circles show exactly where the fold should start and end.

PILOT'S LOG BOOK

Date	Plane	Weather	Take-off speed and angle	Distance (m)	Time (sec)	Average Speed (m/sec)	(km/h)*	Notes

* To calculate your approximate speed in km/h, multiply your speed in metres per second by 3.6.

FLIGHT SCHOOL

While anyone can fly the 12 paper planes in this book, to get the most out of them it's worth spending a little time getting to know your plane and perfecting your flying skills. There are three main areas you can control to make the plane fly to its maximum performance. You need to experiment with all three, remembering that each one affects the other two. One way to keep track of your experiments in aerodynamics is to keep a pilot's log book. Photocopy the template provided and fill it in to track your experiences as a test pilot.

Angle of launch

Most paper planes need to be launched with a slight upward angle. Others prefer a steep angle of launch so they rise rapidly into the air before starting a slow descent. This is especially important if you want to achieve the maximum possible time in the air.

Speed of launch

Every plane has an ideal launch speed, which you can tell only by experimentation. You want to give it forward thrust, but also fly slowly enough for the lift to take effect and not so fast that the wings distort. Generally, planes with shorter wings can be launched faster than those with longer wings.

Trimming

This means adjusting the various parts of the plane. The most important of these is the angle between the wings, known as the 'dihedral'. On most designs, there will be a slight dihedral angle to make the plane more stable. Sometimes, the plane will fly better with a greater angle. With larger sheets of paper, you will need to increase the dihedral to compensate for the extra weight. With standard-sized paper, more subtle adjustments are needed. If one wing is lower than the other, the plane will turn (bank) in that direction. If the wing is more complex, or where there are several wings, adjust them independently.

The other part of the plane that affects flight is the back of the wings (known as the 'trailing edges'). If the plane seems nose-heavy and dives, try curling the back of the wings upwards slightly. Make only small changes, testing each time to see what happens to the flight pattern.

Angle of launch

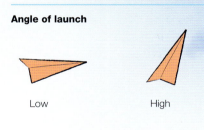

Low   High

Dihedral

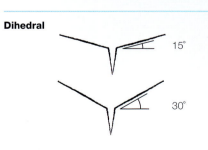

15°

30°

Banking

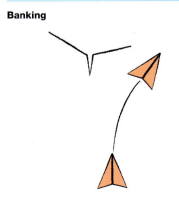

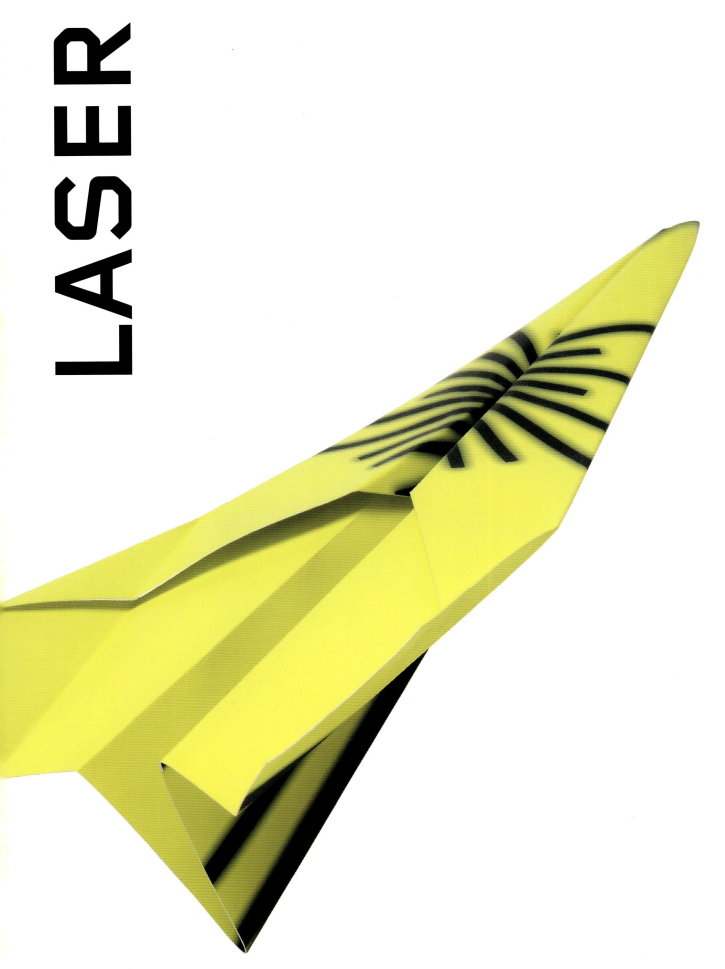

HOW TO BUILD THE LASER

1 Start with a rectangle, with the underside of the plane facing up, creased in half from long side to long side. Fold each half of the top edge to the vertical centre crease.

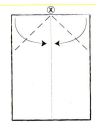

2 Rotate the paper to the right. Fold the angled edges on the right to the centre.

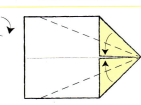

3 This is the result.

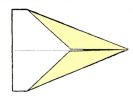

4 Turn the paper over. Fold the long edges to the centre.

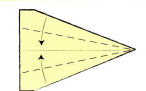

5 Fold the short inside edges to the outer edges.

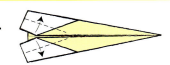

6 Mountain-fold the lower half underneath.

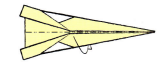

7 Open the wings to match the profile.

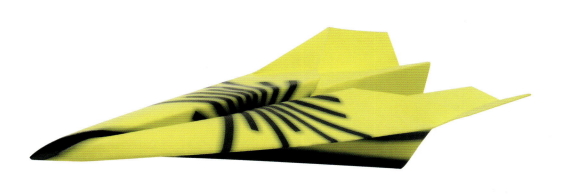

This is a slight variation on a well-known design. Because the wing profile is very narrow, it doesn't generate as much lift as the other designs. The flip side is that it is much more streamlined, so it can travel a very long way, very quickly. The only limitation on distance is the strength of your arm! The plane is used mainly in an ultra-fast transport role, carrying up to four people, including the pilot. In order to land on shorter runways, it is capable of using 100% reverse thrust. It can carry modest weapons, but its raw speed is its best defence. Its narrow profile also gives it very low radar visibility.

Creative Tip If you fold one of the rear stabilizing fins in the opposite direction, you can make the plane rotate as it flies!

PLANE TYPE Fast transport

 LENGTH 490 mm (19¼ in)

 WINGSPAN 150 mm (5⅞ in)

 TAKE-OFF SPEED Fast

 RANGE Medium

LIGHTNING

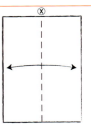

This is a design based on the traditional paper dart, but with some modern extensions to bring it up to date. A pleat is made in the fuselage and the top corners of this pleat are squash-folded to allow the nose cone to be vertical. This is the standard interceptor in use today and the one all pilots use in training. It carries twin synchronized 305 mm (12 in) armour-piercing cannon, which can fire at a rate of 500 rounds per minute. It should be launched at high speed, almost vertically. Trim the plane by adjusting the dihedral (angle of the wings).

Creative Tip Alter the distance of the fold in step 6 and see how it affects the flight pattern.

PLANE TYPE Interceptor

 LENGTH 440 mm (17⅜ in)

 WINGSPAN 165 mm (6½ in)

 TAKE-OFF SPEED Fast

 RANGE Medium

HOW TO BUILD THE LIGHTNING

1 Start with a rectangle, with the underside of the plane facing up, creased in half from long side to long side.

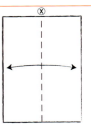

2 Fold the top two corners over to meet the vertical centre crease.

3 Fold the upper edges over again to the vertical centre.

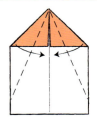

4 This is the result.

5 Turn the paper over. Fold the sides of the wing to the vertical centre, then crease firmly and unfold.

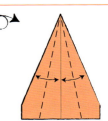

6 Turn back over. Fold the top point down so that the circled areas meet (see step 7).

7 Leave a small gap, then fold the point back up again.

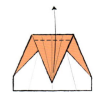

8 Rotate the paper to the left. Fold in half from bottom to top.

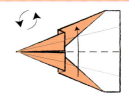

9 Fold the back section of the wing down, squashing the front end into a neat triangle.

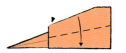

10 This is the result. Repeat on the other wing.

11 Open the wings outwards, leaving the nose section vertical.

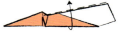

ORCA

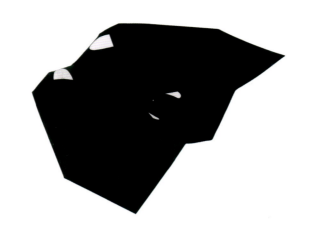

ORCA

This uses the natural geometry of the 'A' rectangle, folding corners to the halfway points. This produces a suitable triangular profile to distribute weight towards the front. The plane is a compact and relatively light design, perfect for close-in dog fights. Because it uses a fuel-hungry, enhanced ion-jet engine, it doesn't have a long range, but it is perfect for use on aircraft carriers or to defend an airbase. It is equipped with Behringer modulated flange weapons, capable of disrupting the internal phase of opposing machines. It should be launched rapidly, at a steep upward angle.

Creative Tip Alter the angle of the wings and the launch angle to see how the two factors interact with each other. Can you make it fly in a circle?

PLANE TYPE Fighter

 LENGTH 305 mm (12 in)

 WINGSPAN 250 mm (9⅞ in)

 TAKE-OFF SPEED Medium

 RANGE Short

HOW TO BUILD THE ORCA

1 Start with a rectangle, with the top of the plane facing up, creased in half from long side to long side. Fold in half from side to side, then crease and unfold.
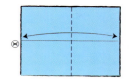

2 Fold the left edge to the centre, then crease and unfold.

3 Turn the paper over. Fold the two circled points to meet, then crease and unfold.

4 Make the same fold from the opposite side.
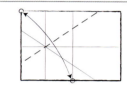

5 Use only the existing creases to collapse the paper, interlocking the layers in any way you want.
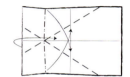

6 Fold the triangular corner to the right.
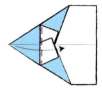

7 Leave a small gap, then fold the triangle back to the left.
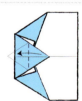

8 Mountain-fold the lower half underneath.
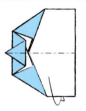

9 Fold both wings down to match the dotted line.

10 Fold the wings back to match the profile.

HOW TO BUILD THE RAPTOR

1 Start with a rectangle, with the underside of the plane facing up, creased in half from long side to long side. Fold the top edge over to the right edge, making a gentle pinch-mark on the centre crease. Unfold again.

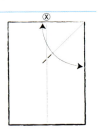

2 Fold the top edge down to the pinch mark.

3 Fold the top-left corner to touch where the coloured edge meets the vertical centre crease.

4 Unfold the flap and repeat on the right side.

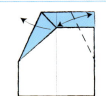

5 Make a crease, starting at each top corner that meets the existing crease where it passes through the coloured edge (circled).

6 Fold the left-hand flap over, tucking the small triangular flap under the coloured layer.

7 Mountain-fold the left half of the plane underneath.

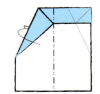

8 Fold the top-left corner over, making a crease starting at the lower left corner of the coloured area, meeting the top end of an existing crease.

9 Repeat step 6, tucking the small triangular flap under the layers.

10 Turn the paper to the right. Fold the lower edge to meet the upper edge on the right, extending the crease to a point near the top-left corner. Repeat on the underside.

11 Fold the wingtip back to meet the lower edge. Repeat on the other side.

12 Open the wings to match the profile.

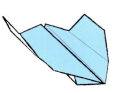

This plane has been created to provide wings with a relatively large surface area, maximizing lift. It uses stealth technology to make it invisible to radar, allowing it to hang in the air above the target, then descend at high speed to release a deadly packet of ionic bombs. These weapons are designed to knock out all electronic devices within a 10 km (6 mile) radius, but without harming people. Launch mode should be steady, at a slight upward angle, ideally from the top of a skyscraper.

Creative Tip The folding sequence incorporates some clever technology at steps 9 and 10 to 'lock' the nose of the plane together. Could you use this technique on other planes? It's much better than using sticky tape!

PLANE TYPE Bomber

 LENGTH 405 mm (16 in)

 WINGSPAN 240 mm (9½ in)

 TAKE-OFF SPEED Fast

 RANGE Medium

HOW TO BUILD THE HORNET

1 Start with a rectangle, with the underside of the plane facing up, creased in half from long side to long side. Mark the centre point by folding the two short edges together and gently pinching.

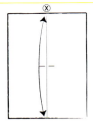

2 Turn the paper to the right. Fold the upper and lower edges to the centre, creasing and unfolding each time.

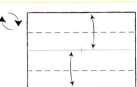

3 Fold the right-hand edge to the centre mark.

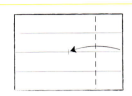

4 Starting at the right, fold the lower corner to lie on the circled crease.

5 Fold the upper right edge over the lower section.

6 Reinforce the horizontal crease through all layers on the right-hand side.

7 Fold the tip on the right to meet the centre.

8 Fold the triangular flap over the edge of the folded tip, then crease and unfold.

9 Tuck the flap into the pocket of the folded tip and flatten the paper.

10 Mountain-fold the lower half underneath.

11 Fold the upper edge to meet the lower edge. Repeat on the other side.

12 Open the wings to match the profile.

This is a design that uses ultra-modern 60-degree geometry in the folding sequence. Because the resulting wings and fuselage are relatively simple in structure, this plane can be folded quickly and can withstand a lot of enemy firepower. It is best launched at high speed to break through enemy defences and inflict real damage on the opposition before they have a chance to react. However, it is also capable of slower flight by increasing the dihedral (angle of the wings). The main weapon is a set of six GOB/LA-9 synchronized rotary cannons, one of the largest, heaviest and most powerful aircraft cannon available today.

Creative Tip Try altering the angle of the wings (see step 11) to see how it affects the flight pattern.

PLANE TYPE Ground attack

 LENGTH 280 mm (11 in)

 WINGSPAN 165 mm (6½ in)

 TAKE-OFF SPEED Fast

 RANGE Short

VIPER

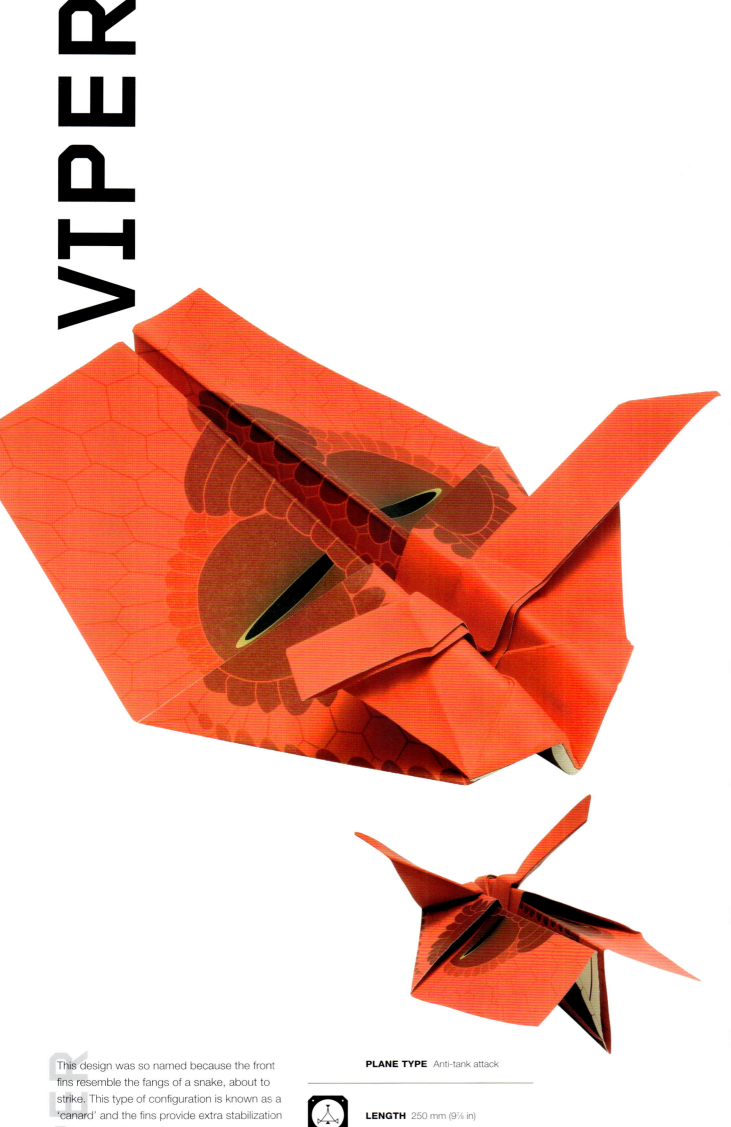

VIPER

This design was so named because the front fins resemble the fangs of a snake, about to strike. This type of configuration is known as a 'canard' and the fins provide extra stabilization during flight. The move at step 4 is known in the origami world as a 'water-bomb base'. The plane is a nimble aerobatic design; by adjusting the fins, you can create many unusual flight patterns. The plane is usually equipped with Morpheus anti-tank pods, capable of immobilizing the tank and crew for capture by ground forces.

Creative Tip Alter the distance of the fold in step 5. What effect will this have?

PLANE TYPE Anti-tank attack

 LENGTH 250 mm (9⅞ in)

 WINGSPAN 245 mm (9⅝ in)

 TAKE-OFF SPEED Medium

 RANGE Short

HOW TO BUILD THE VIPER

1 Start with a rectangle, with the underside of the plane facing up, creased in half from side to side.
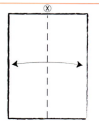

2 Fold the top edges to lie on the left and right sides. Crease, then unfold.
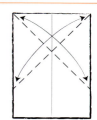

3 Turn the paper over. Fold the top corners to lie on the lower creases. Crease, then unfold.
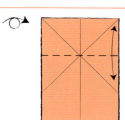

4 Turn the paper back over and use the creases to collapse the paper.
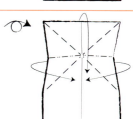

5 Fold the top corner about two-thirds of the way down.
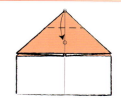

6 Fold the original top edge upwards, carefully squashing the inside corners into neat triangles.
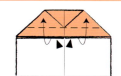

7 Fold in half from right to left.
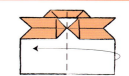

8 Fold the wings over on each side, so that the circled points meet.

9 Fold the 'fin' over on each side, so that two folded edges meet.

10 Open the wings and fins to match the profile.
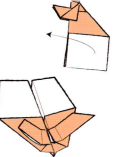

HOW TO BUILD THE MANTA

1 Start with a rectangle, with the underside of the plane facing up, creased in half from long side to long side. Fold two corners over to lie on the centre crease.

2 Fold the triangular section down.

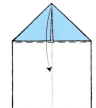

3 Turn the paper over. As in step 1, fold the top corners to the centre crease.

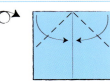

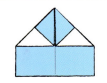

4 This is the result.

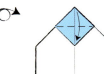

5 Turn the paper over. Fold the square flap in half downwards.

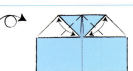

6 Turn the paper over. Fold the inner corners outwards, then crease and unfold.

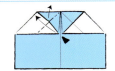

7 Squash the left point out, opening up the paper into a new position.

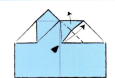

8 Repeat on the right-hand side.

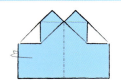

9 Mountain-fold the left half underneath.

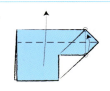

10 Turn the paper to the right. Fold both wings upwards, so that the circled points meet.

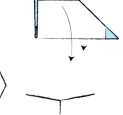

11 Open the wings to match the profile.

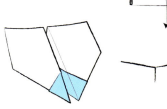

Unusually for a paper plane, this design features two 'prongs' at the front end, similar to a manta ray. The origami technique known as 'squashing' is used to create them. It is an all-weather reconnaissance plane which is also capable of launching attacks. The sting in the tail of this design is a phase-looped induction coil, which can launch a 150-kilojoule electromagnetic pulse at other aircraft, toppling their internal gyro systems and causing them to crash spectacularly. You should launch with moderate speed, at a slight upward angle. Experiment with the dihedral for optimum results.

Creative Tip What happens if you fold the flap further or less far down in step 5? How does it affect the next step?

PLANE TYPE Reconnaissance/attack

 LENGTH 280 mm (11 in)

 WINGSPAN 245 mm (9⅝ in)

 TAKE-OFF SPEED Slow

 RANGE Medium

HOW TO BUILD THE SWALLOW

1 Start with a rectangle, with the top of the plane facing up, creased in half from long side to long side. Fold the two short edges together.

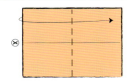

2 Fold the top and bottom edges to the centre crease.

3 Fold the two corners of the left flaps to meet the outside edges.

4 Lift up the lower flap slightly and ease out the first layer from inside. Flatten into a neat triangle.

5 Repeat on the upper side.

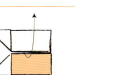

6 Swing the central flap to the left.

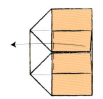

7 Fold the end of the flap underneath, making a firm crease, then unfold the flap back to the right.

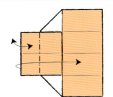

8 Refold the flap, tucking its ends into the two small pockets.

9 Turn the paper over. Fold the lower edge of the wing to the opposite quarter crease. Crease firmly, then unfold. Repeat the fold on the opposite side.

10 Fold the lower edge of the wing to the nearest quarter crease. Crease firmly, then unfold. Repeat the fold on the opposite side.

11 Turn the paper over. Crease as shown and adjust the paper to match the profile.

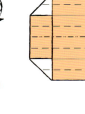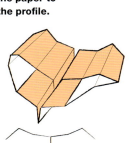

This design is among the most aerobatic in the book and is based on a traditional origami design called the 'Japanese house'. The pleats in the wings make it very stable, so you can launch the plane at any speed or angle, as hard as you like. The plane is quite an old design and is not suited to modern combat conditions, so it is used for training new pilots and for extraordinary displays at airshows. It is capable of making a 25G turn, with the pilot requiring oxygen in order to stay conscious!

Creative Tip Experiment with the many possible wing profiles.

PLANE TYPE Trainer

 LENGTH 245 mm (9⅝ in)

 WINGSPAN 220 mm (8⅝ in)

 TAKE-OFF SPEED Medium

 RANGE Long

HOW TO BUILD THE SKUA

1 Start with a rectangle, with the top side of the plane facing up. Crease in half from long side to long side, then unfold.

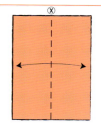

2 Fold the two upper corners over to lie along the vertical centre crease.

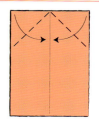

3 Turn the paper over. Fold the upper edges to the vertical centre, allowing flaps of paper to pop out from underneath.

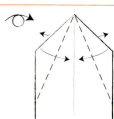

4 Fold the square at the top in half.

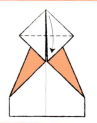

5 Leave a small gap, then fold the point back upwards.

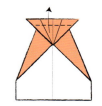

6 Fold the top of the paper to the centre of the bottom edge.

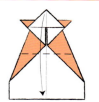

7 Leave another small gap and fold the paper back upwards.

8 Mountain-fold the right side underneath.

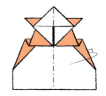

9 Fold the wings over so the circled edges line up.

10 Open the wings to match the profile.

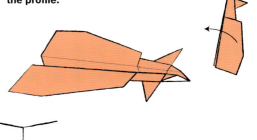

This design is an example of the 'canard' configuration, with smaller stabilizing wings located at the front of the plane. Properly adjusted, they provide a lot of subtle control over the flight characteristics. The Skua is a dive-bomber, designed to hover in the skies while using epsilon radar technology mounted in the canard wings to locate its prey. It then descends at high speed to hit the designated target. This model is the long-range version, capable of flying round the world without refuelling. By setting the front stabilizers at different angles, you can allow the plane to slowly arc left or right.

Creative Tip Try moving the location of the fold in step 6 – how does it affect the flight pattern?

PLANE TYPE Dive bomber

 LENGTH 395 mm (15½ in)

 WINGSPAN 180 mm (7⅛ in)

 TAKE-OFF SPEED Medium

 RANGE Long

IMPALA

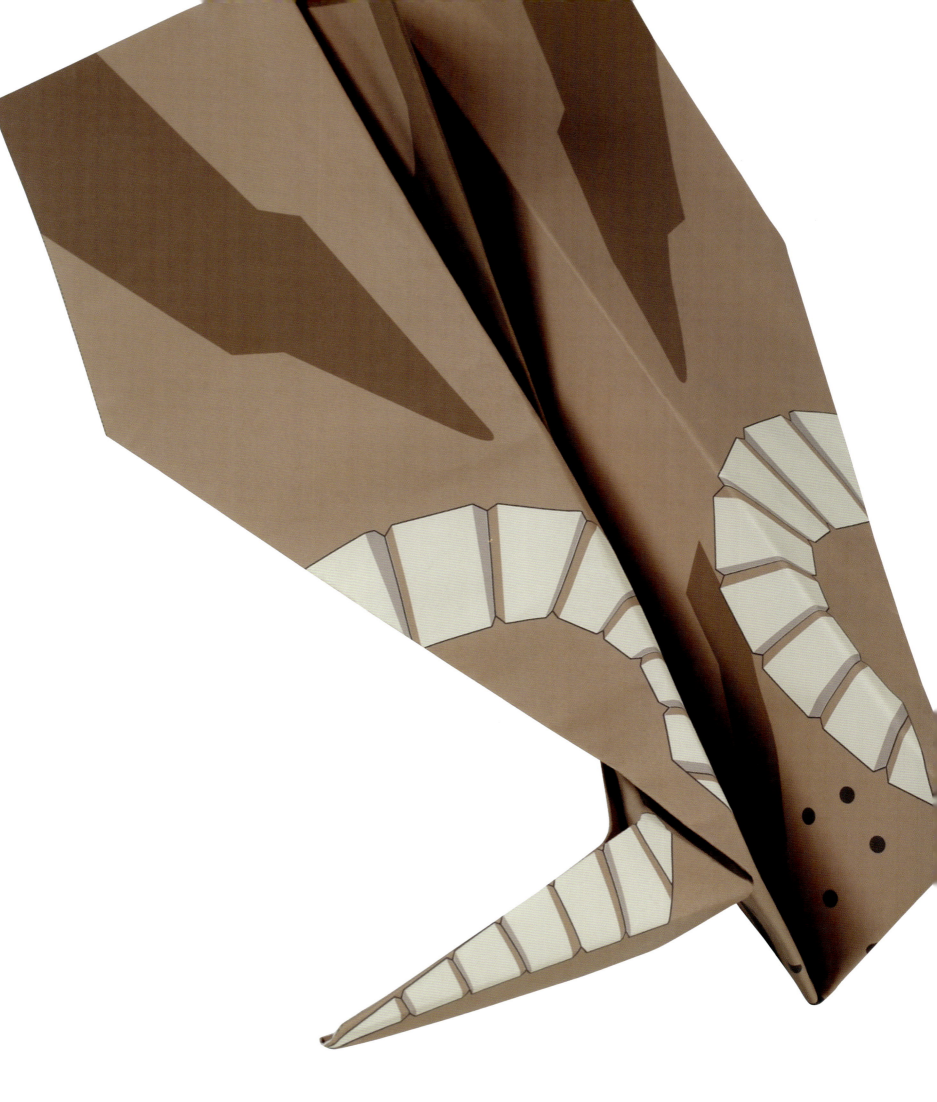

This model uses 60-degree geometry in its construction, allowing for radically new techniques to be used. This does require you to be very accurate when making the creases in steps 1 and 3. The 'horns' of this design make use of the equilateral triangles formed by the creases. This fighter is sleek and fast, capable of flying long distances. It is likely to become the standard military fighter within the next few years. It incorporates the latest pulse-disruptor beam designs in each of the horns. These cause metal joints to vibrate apart, so the enemy literally drops out of the sky.

Creative Tip Try folding more or less paper to form the tail fin in step 15. Is it more stable? What happens if you bend the horns at different angles?

PLANE TYPE Fighter

 LENGTH 295 mm (11⅝ in)

 WINGSPAN 185 mm (7¼ in)

 TAKE-OFF SPEED Fast

 RANGE Medium

HOW TO BUILD THE IMPALA

1 Start with a rectangle, with the underside of the plane uppermost, creased in half from long side to long side. Starting the crease at the bottom-left corner, fold the lower right corner to touch the vertical crease.

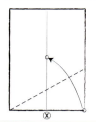

2 This is the result. Unfold the flap.

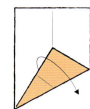

3 Repeat on the right side.

4 Turn the paper over. Fold the lower corners to the opposite ends of the creases. Crease and unfold.

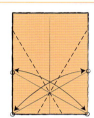

5 Collapse the paper using only the existing creases.

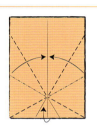

6 Fold the outer coloured edges to the vertical centre, then crease and unfold.

7 Fold the outer edge to the nearest crease and edge. Crease and unfold. Repeat on the three matching areas.

8 Fold the lower triangular section in half upwards.

9 Open and squash the lower right flap inwards.

10 Push in the sides of the narrow flap using the existing creases.

11 Fold the flap outwards.

12 Fold the flap in half. Repeat steps 9–12 on the other side.

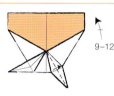

13 Mountain-fold the left side underneath.

14 Turn the paper to the left. Fold the upper edge of the wing to the lower edge, then crease and unfold. Repeat on the other side.

15 Make a crease between the circled points, then unfold.

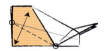

16 Push in the lower corner.

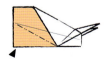

17 Fold the wings down to match the profile.

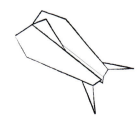

This plane is of Danish origin and was created by a former supersonic test pilot. It uses unusual folding techniques to create a vertical fin which allows for very good lateral stability. The proportions in step 3 are a guide only – look at the drawing in step 4 and use your eyes to guide you. The Hunter (the original Danish name is 'Jagerfly') is a light bomber capable of carrying up to 500 kg (1,100 lbs). This will usually consist of a combination of bombs, missiles and incendiary weapons, although it can be modified for many different purposes. It is best flown with simultaneous tactical support from some of the lighter escort machines.

Creative Tip The flap formed in step 16 has many creative possibilities – what else can you do with it?

PLANE TYPE Light bomber

LENGTH 220 mm (8⅝ in)

WINGSPAN 210 mm (8¼ in)

TAKE-OFF SPEED Fast

RANGE Long

HOW TO BUILD THE HUNTER

1 Start with a rectangle, with the underside of the plane facing up. Fold the short edges together.
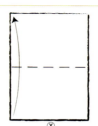

2 Crease in half from side to side and unfold.
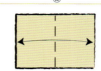

3 Fold the lower left corner to the position shown. Use the divided rulers as guidance.

4 This is the result.

5 Turn the paper over and fold the left half of the paper to the right.
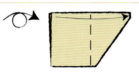

6 Fold the lower right corner to match the layer underneath. The circled corners meet.

7 Open the lower layer to the left.

8 Fold the upper inside edge to the outer edge, then crease and unfold.

9 Fold the lower inside edge to the outer edge, then crease and unfold.

10 Unfold the left flap.
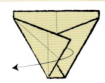

11 Crease the bisector of the lower left corner. Repeat steps 8–11 on the other side.
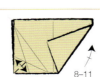

12 Squash the corner using the existing creases.
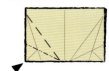

13 Fold the sides in, pressing the point downwards into a triangle. You'll need to make a new valley crease to do this.

14 This is the result. Repeat steps 12–14 on the other side.

15 Turn the paper over from top to bottom. Crease the bisectors of the outer corners.
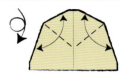

16 Lift the two sides up to form a vertical flap in the centre.

17 Flatten the flap to both sides.

18 Fold the corner of the flap inwards.
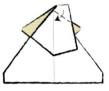

19 Fold the same flap over again, taking the crease to the lower corner.

20 Fold the left half over to the right.
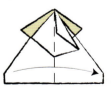

21 Fold both wings down along an inside folded edge and adjust them to match the profile.

TEMKO

HOW TO BUILD THE TEMKO

1 Start with a rectangle, with the underside of the plane facing up, creased in half from long side to long side. Fold the upper edge to both left and right edges, then crease and unfold.

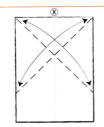

2 Turn the paper over. Fold the upper edge to the ends of the creases. Crease and unfold.

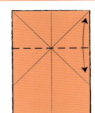

3 Turn the paper back over and collapse it using only the existing creases.

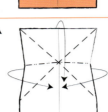

4 Fold the upper left flap to the right.

5 Fold the left edge to the vertical centre.

6 Fold the edge out to match the dotted position. The circled points meet.

7 Fold the upper edge of the small coloured triangle to the lower inside edge.

8 Fold the upper left edge in, creasing between the two circles.

9 Fold two flaps on the right over to the left.

10 Repeat steps 5–8 on the right-hand side.

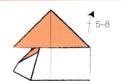

11 Fold the top corner down, so that the circled points meet.

12 Using the dividers as a guide, fold the point back upwards.

13 Mountain-fold the right half underneath.

14 Turn the paper to the right. Fold the lower left corner over, creasing between the circled points. Unfold again.

15 Push the lower corner in using the crease you've just made.

16 Fold the wings down, creasing between the left and right corners. Adjust them to match the profile.

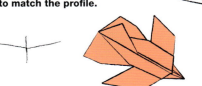

This is the most advanced design in the book, requiring you to pay close attention to the diagrams. It was designed by Florence Temko, a prolific and friendly origami author. The technique in steps 14 and 15 can be applied to many other designs, although it won't always make them fly better! The Temko is a medium-sized bomber that has taken over from the F14 in the United States Air Force. It is lighter and therefore more manoeuvrable. As well as a wide range of bombs, it carries a Schmitt-Drewien cannon that sends pulses of sonic energy to take out the opponent.

Creative Tip Alter the angle of the tail fins in step 7. Try different angles on the front and rear wings.

 PLANE TYPE Bomber

LENGTH 245 mm (9⅝ in)

 WINGSPAN 240 mm (9½ in)

 TAKE-OFF SPEED Medium

 RANGE Short

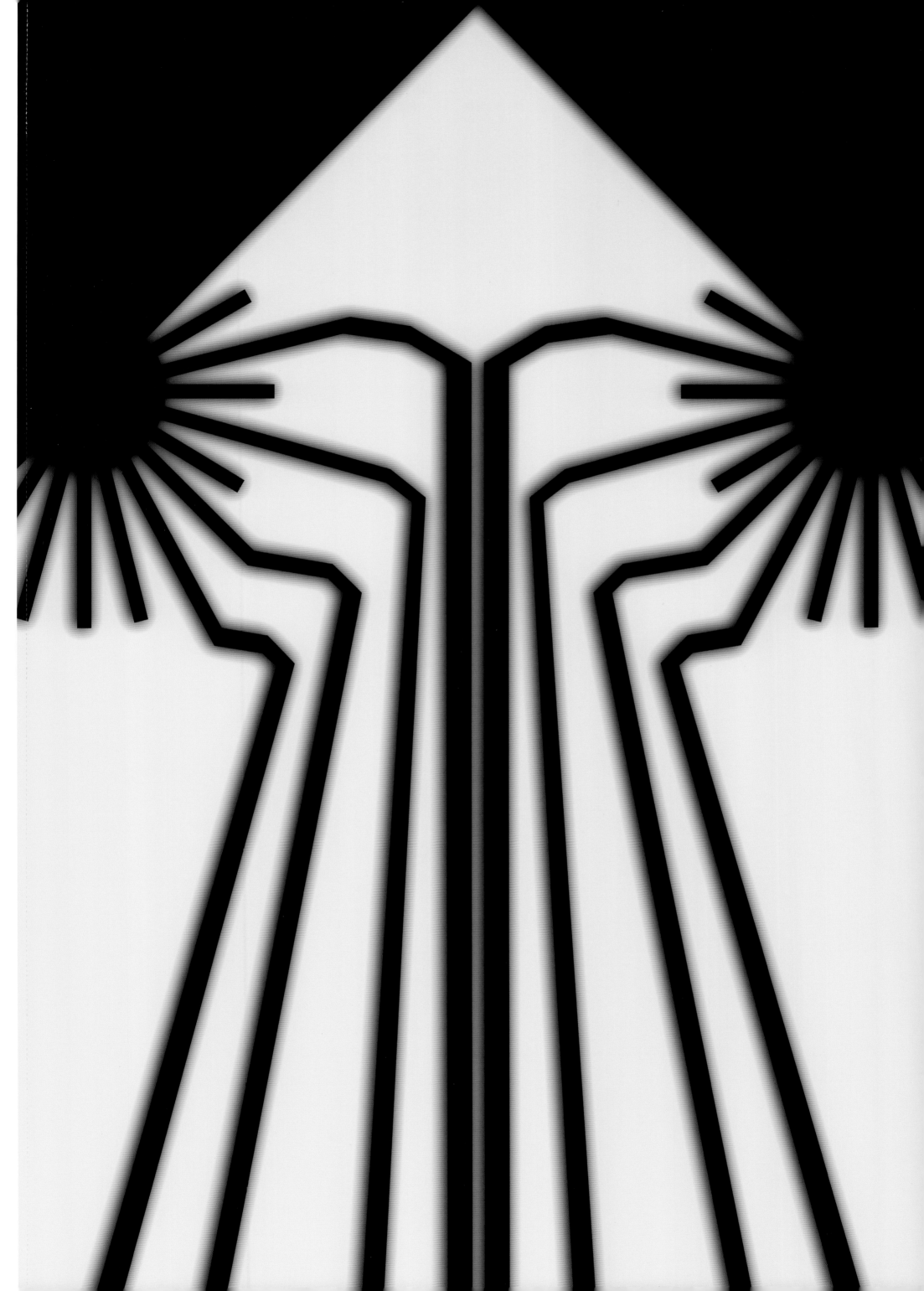

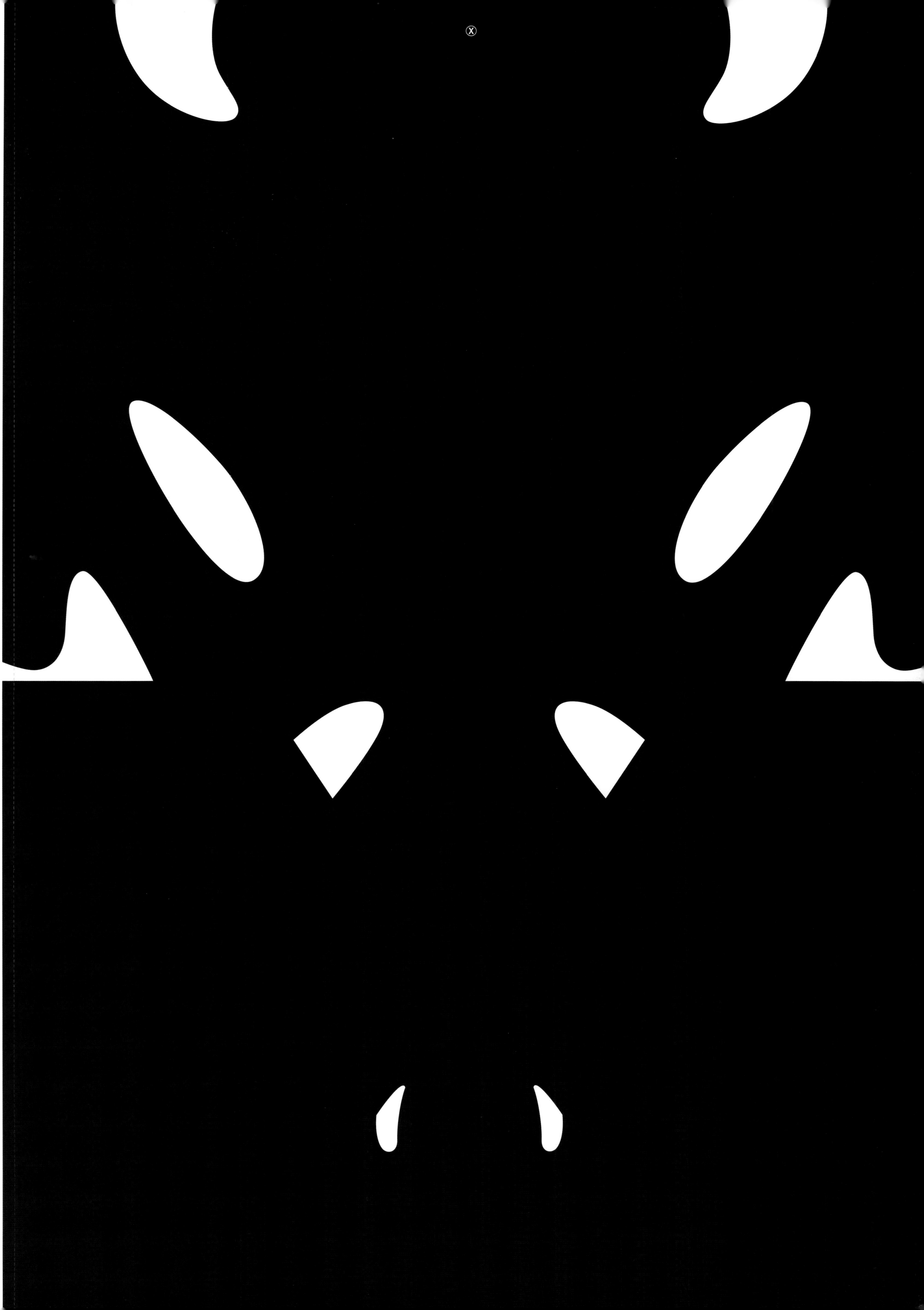

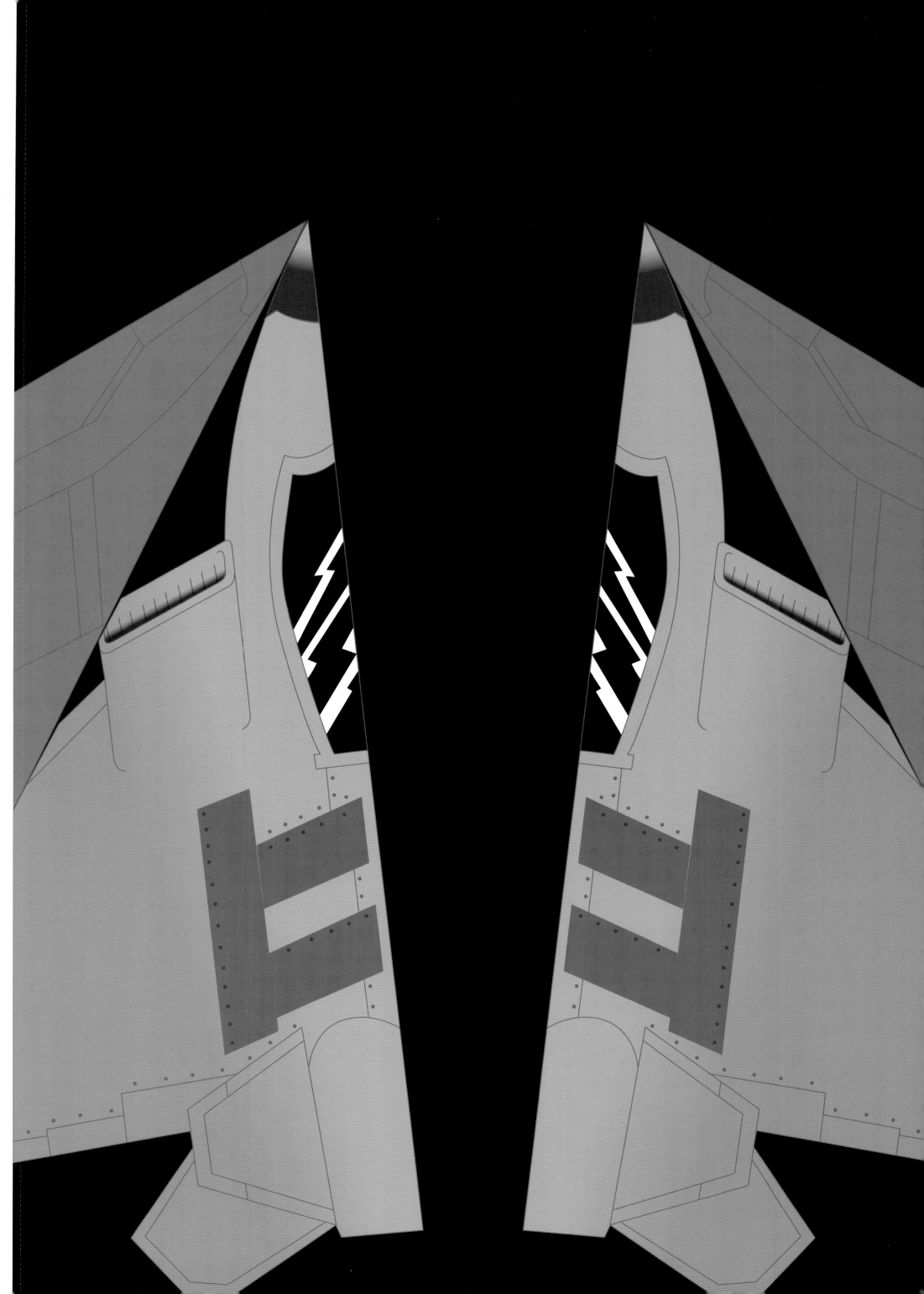

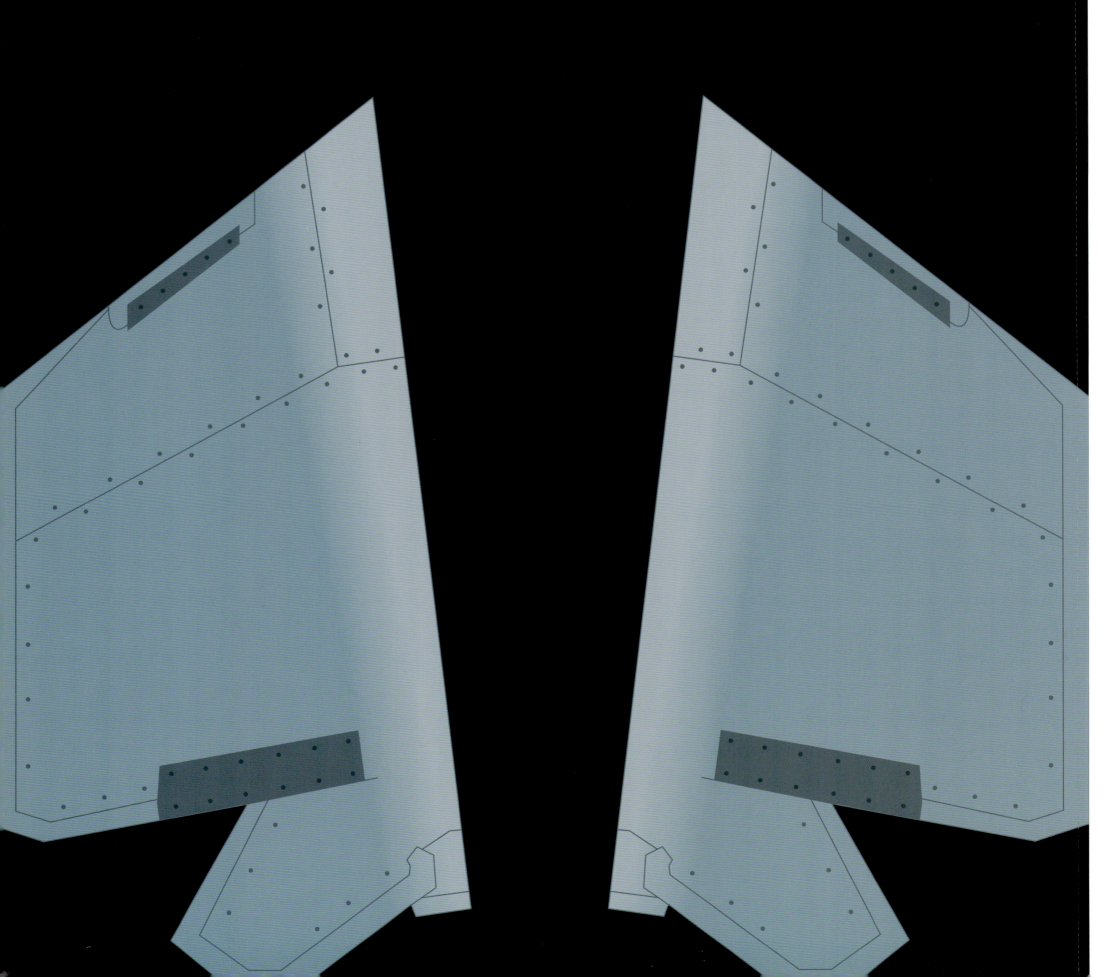

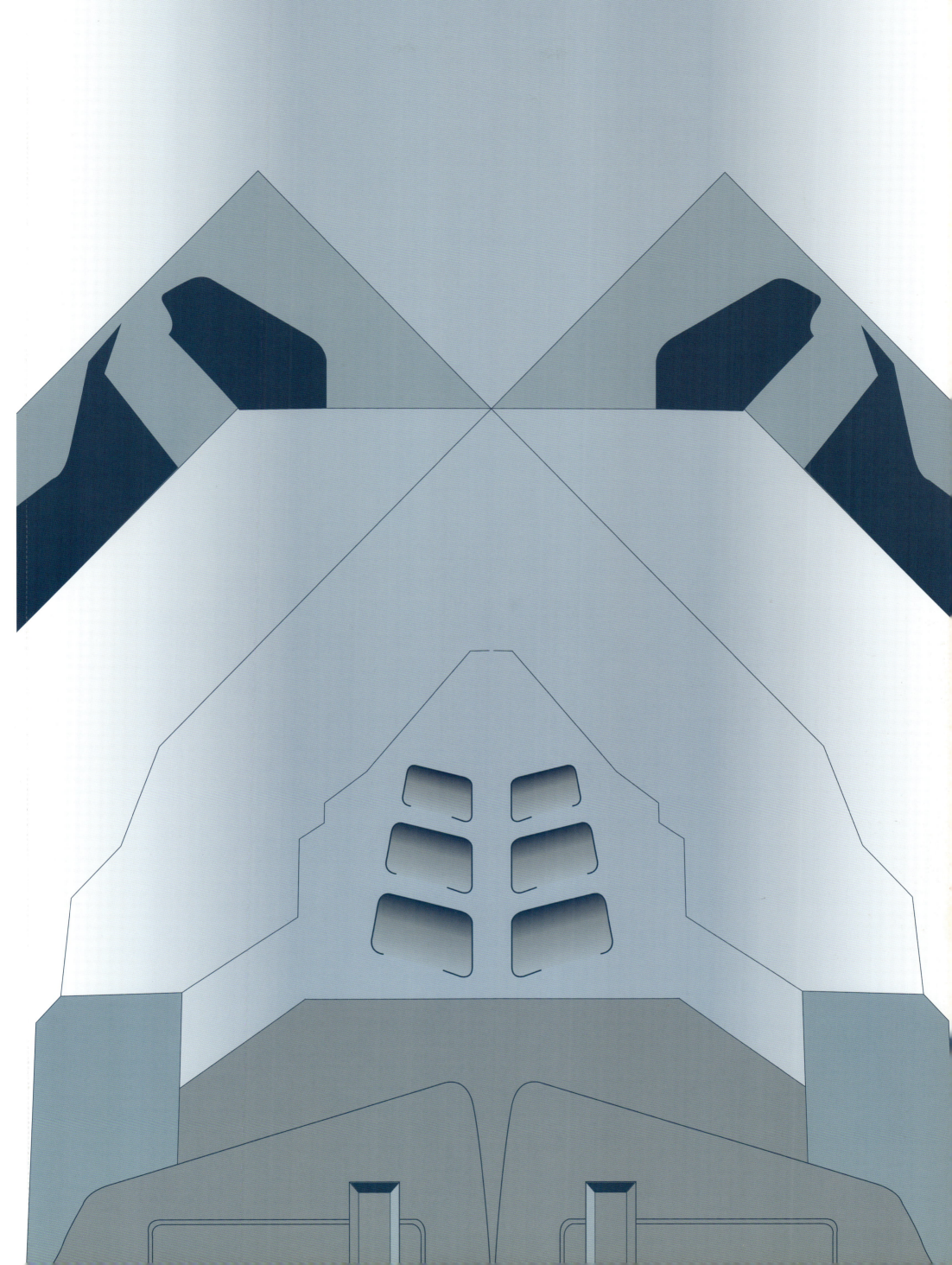

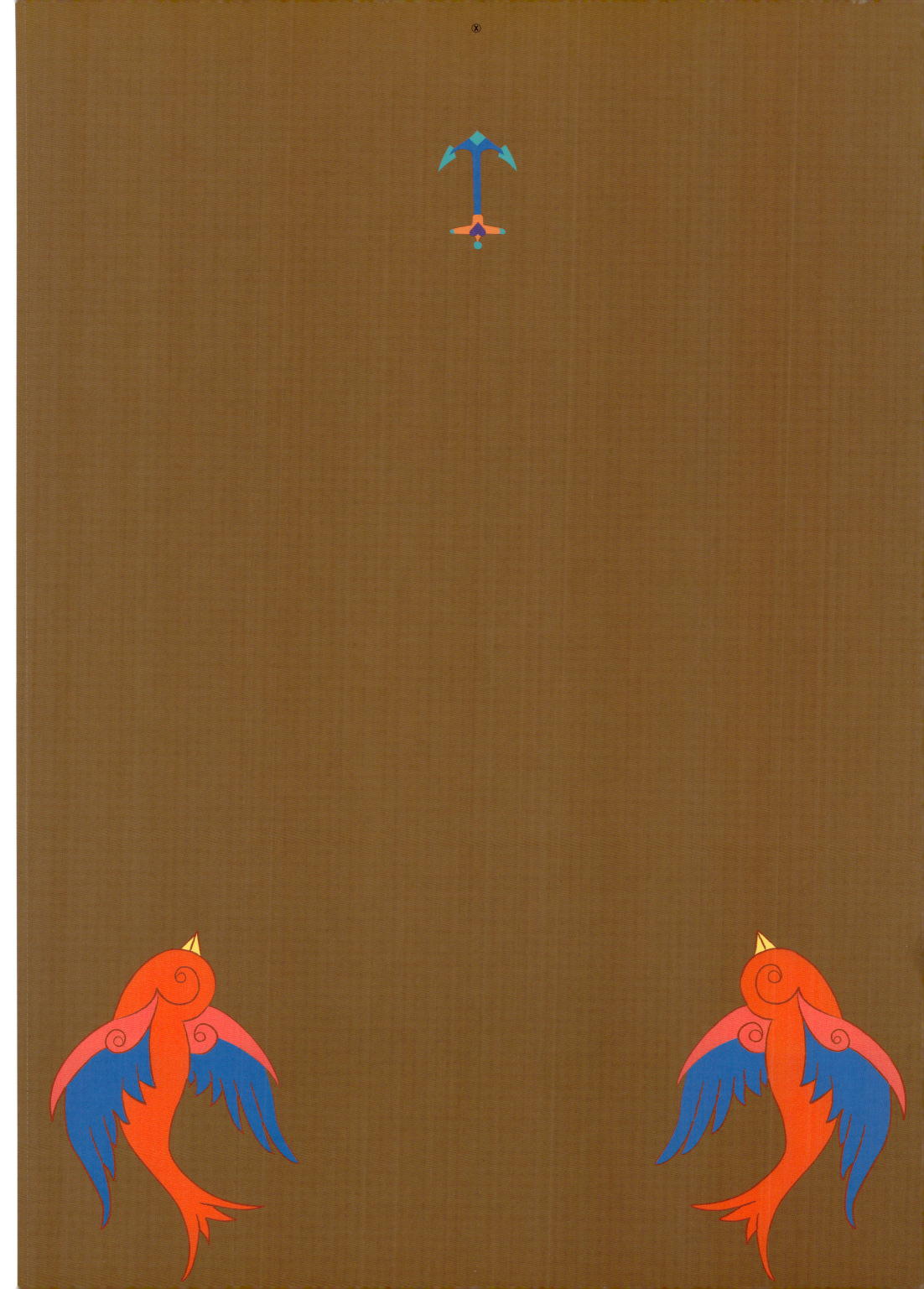

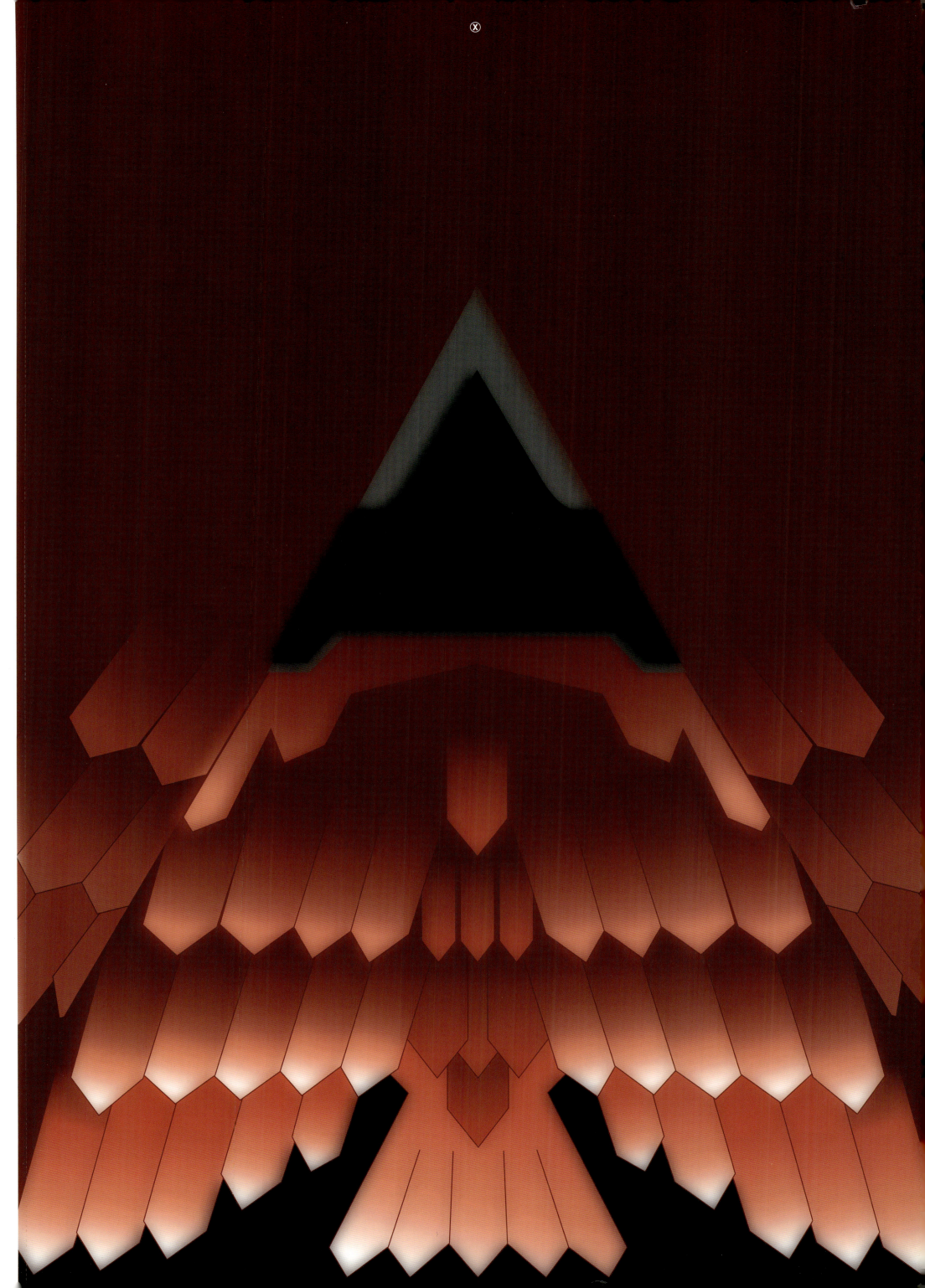